The

Stay WISE My Friends!

MONTH_____ YEAR _____

Brian,

Stay WISE my Friend!

www.wisdomjournal.org

Publishers Disclaimer

"Scripture taken from the NEW AMERICAN STANDARD BIBLE®, © Copyright 1960, 1962, 1963, 1968, 1971, 1972, 1973, 1975, 1977, 1995 by The Lockman Foundation Used by permission." www.Lockman.org

First Edition
ISBN: 9798794432312

www.wisdomjournal.org

CONGRATULATIONS!
ANOTHER MONTH OF WISDOM

FOR COPIES OF THE WISDOM JOURNAL
SUBSCRIBE FOR MONTHLY JOURNAL DELIVERY
ORDER JOURNALS FOR SMALL GROUP BIBLE STUDY
PARTICIPATE IN AN UPCOMING WISDOM WORKSHOP
JOIN MONTHLY WISDOM FOR LIFE MASTERMIND GROUP

GO TO WWW.WISDOMJOURNAL.ORG

The Wisdom Journal

Stay WISE My Friends!

www.wisdomjournal.org

DEDICATION

To my mom & dad,
my brothers & sisters, my children,
colleagues, coaches, family members, friends,
mentors, partners, pastors, teachers, & *Sandra My Love*.
Each one of you has blessed my life with wisdom & wonder.

Stay WISE My Friends!

~ Marc Feinberg

Wisdom is the principle thing, therefore get wisdom

~ Proverbs 4:7

Table of Contents

My son, do not let wisdom
and understanding out of your sight

~Proverbs 3:21

www.wisdomjournal.org

Why Wisdom?

All of us want to create love and connection, optimize health, build substantial wealth, create inner peace, live on purpose, live with passion, experience greater fulfillment, and have a significant impact, influence, and contribution to humanity.

Some of us need to return to God, restore our relationships, and reignite our purpose in life.

Many of us just need a daily disciple studying God's word more consistently.

All of us want to live our best life now and become the best version of ourselves in every area of our life.

Inside "31 WISE" you will discover wisdom for everyday life, the wisdom necessary to make right choices and life changing decisions, as you journal and journey your way through the book of proverbs.

By deciding to pursue God's wisdom, you've made a commitment to bless and obey God, to honor yourself, and to share your wisdom with others.

The wisdom found in the book of Proverbs is a lamp for your feet and a light for your path, giving you a clear concise roadmap to living in victory each day.

Experience the wisdom of God, the favor of God, the power of God, and the blessing of God, by seeking the wisdom of God revealed in 31 WISE.

www.wisdomjournal.org

For the Lord gives wisdom: from his mouth come knowledge and understanding

~Proverbs 2:6

The Original "Wise Guy"

"The Power of Wisdom"

In the bible, 1Kings 3:1-14 is a perfect illustration of the wonders of wisdom and the power of God working through wisdom, in the life of King Solomon, the wisest and wealthiest man to ever live.

1Then Solomon formed a marriage alliance with Pharaoh king of Egypt, and took Pharaoh's daughter and brought her to the city of David until he had finished building his own house and the house of the Lord and the wall around Jerusalem. 2The people were still sacrificing on the high places, because there was no house built for the name of the Lord until those days. 3Now Solomon loved the Lord, walking in the statutes of his father David, except he sacrificed and burned incense on the high places. 4The king went to Gibeon to sacrifice there, for that was the great high place; Solomon offered a thousand burnt offerings on that altar. 5In Gibeon the Lord appeared to Solomon in a dream at night; and God said, "Ask what *you wish* Me to give you."

6Then Solomon said, "You have shown great lovingkindness to Your servant David my father, according as he walked before You in truth and righteousness and uprightness of heart toward You; and You have reserved for him this great lovingkindness, that You have given him a son to sit on his throne, as *it is* this day. 7Now, O Lord my God, You have made Your servant king in place of my father David, yet I am but a little child; I do not know how to go out or come in. 8Your servant is in the midst of Your people which You have chosen, a great people who are too many to be numbered or counted.

9**So give Your servant an understanding heart to judge Your people to discern between good and evil. For who is able to judge this great people of Yours?"** 10It was pleasing in the sight of the Lord that Solomon had asked this thing. 11God said to him, "Because you have asked this thing and have not asked for yourself long life, nor have asked riches for yourself, nor have you asked for the life of your enemies, but have asked for yourself discernment to understand justice,

12behold, I have done according to your words.

Behold, I have given you a wise and discerning heart, so that there has been no one like you before you, nor shall one like you arise after you. 13I have also given you what you have not asked, both riches and honor, so that there will not be any among the kings like you all your days.

14If you walk in My ways, keeping My statutes and commandments, as your father David walked, then I will prolong your days."

Commit to the Lord whatever you do,
and he will establish your plans.

~ Proverbs 16:3

What Is
The Wisdom Journal?

The Wisdom Journal is *__a powerful timeless tool__* to obtain wisdom for your life as you journey each day through the Proverbs using "The W.I.S.E. Method".

The Wisdom Journal is *__a simple system__* for you to discover God's wisdom, encouraging you to make wiser choices and even life changing decisions.

The Wisdom Journal is *__an effective way to execute__* and create outstanding outcomes in the areas of faith, family, friendship, fitness, finance, career, contribution, purpose, destiny, and legacy.

The Wisdom Journal is *__a method of accountability__* to increase personal and professional productivity. We recommend that your spouse, partner, colleague, friend, or family member join along with you on your journey to discover wisdom for their own life. You can hold each other accountable and form a mastermind alliance to accomplish your dreams and goals faster than ever before.

The Wisdom Journal *__includes all 31 Proverbs__* from the New American Standard Bible. The Wisdom Journal is your journaling system to discover God's wisdom for your life, each day.

The fear of the LORD is the beginning of knowledge,
but fools despise wisdom and instruction.

~ Proverbs 1:7

What Is
The W.I.S.E. Method?

The W.I.S.E. Method is a simple <u>daily discipline,</u> to discover God's Wisdom for your everyday life.

The W.I.S.E. Method

❖ <u>**W**isdom for Today (choose your verse)</u>

❖ <u>**I**nterpretation for Today (journal your insights)</u>

❖ <u>**S**trategy for Today (create your battle plan)</u>

❖ <u>**E**valuation for Today (reflect on your results)</u>

The wise woman builds her house but
with her own hands the foolish one tears hers down

~ Proverbs 9:10

How to Use
The W.I.S.E. Method

The **W.I.S.E. Method** was created for you to easily experience wisdom for your life in **3+1 simple steps.**

For your personal time of devotion, whatever day of the month it is, turn to that proverb to read, study, journal, and discover the wisdom that you are specifically seeking.

❖ **Wisdom for Today**
In this section you will write down your verse(s) that stands out to you during your daily devotion time in the book of Proverbs.

❖ **Interpretation for Today**
In this section you will journal your thoughts and insights, reflecting on what God is revealing to you about your key verse(s).

❖ **Strategy for Today**
In this section you will prepare a strategy to allow your key verse(s) to influence your thinking, and your actions. Write down executable tactics to create your specific desired outcome.

❖ **Evaluation for Today**
In this section you will evaluate your daily achievements at the end of each day. Remember to celebrate your victories immediately and make any necessary adjustments in your strategy for the next day.

Example: Day

Proverbs 1
~ Day ~

❖ <u>**Wisdom for Today**</u>

Verse 23. Surely, I will pour out my spirit on you; I will make my words known to you.

❖ <u>**Interpretation for Today**</u>

The spirit of wisdom wants ME! Yes, wisdom wants me to know what she is saying, and she wants me to live from that state of knowledge and understanding. Wisdom has many things to share with me and I must be still enough and quiet enough to hear and listen to wisdoms voice and the direction that she has for me today.

❖ <u>**Strategy for Today**</u>

Today I will be in full connection to the spirit of wisdom. I will listen to my self-talk intently so that I am continuously hearing the voice of wisdom. I will consistently master my thoughts and my ability to hear the voice of wisdom as I go through the day instead of allowing the lies and my negative thinking to run my life.

Date: 01/01/2020

Example: Night

Proverbs 1
~ Night ~

❖ **Evaluation for Today**

I was supercharged from the moment I woke up this morning and I just knew that it was going to be a great day! A new year, a fresh perspective and away we go. Feeling accomplished for mapping out my personal goals for love, health and wealth today as well as my vision for this new journey in the church.

I was filled with gratitude all day today. I am clear about the direction of my life this new year. I prayed for all of my family members to optimize their lives and experience fulfillment and significance this year too.

I am going to use my gift as an educator and as a motivator this year to help my brothers and sisters in the world to be fully equipped with Wisdom for Life. I will position The Wisdom Journal as the #1 leading resource ever created for spiritual growth & development.

Thank you, Lord! I love you, Lord!

Trust in the Lord with all of your heart
An lean not on your own understanding
In all your ways acknowledge Him,
And He shall direct your paths

~Proverbs 3:5-6

The Wisdom Foreword

By Pastor John Chinelly
Calvary Chapel Fort Lauderdale

My journey with the Lord started the day I was born-again in 1977. As a new believer, I began to read and study the scriptures daily. The Book of Proverbs immediately caught my attention and captivated me. I've committed to reading a chapter a day since.

There are 31 total chapters in the Book of Proverbs, a chapter of wisdom for every day. The Book of Proverbs radically impacted my life, and the wisdom contained within its rich principles ignited my heart and mind to levels of truth and understanding I could only dream of.

As a Pastor and Biblical Counselor, I rely upon the verses found in The Book of Proverbs to bring wisdom, life, hope, healing, counsel, advice, insight and direction to those in need.

The two verses found in Proverbs 3:5-6 have become my "life verses," continuously providing me with countless opportunities to assist others who are seeking the Lord to overcome the challenges & the issues of their everyday life.

The Lord Jesus Christ has guided my life and path these past 40 years. Through the book of Proverbs, I have found the Lord influencing my life down the path of His leading. In all 31 chapters I have discovered a wealth of truth and knowledge found nowhere else in my entire life.

I invite you to join me on this glorious journey to know God and the truth of his word. I encourage you to use 31 Wise as a tool and a daily discipline to discover the necessary wisdom for your everyday life. God bless you in your search for daily wisdom and may the Spirit of the Lord give you His wisdom and revelation from now until eternity.

Love In Christ
John Chinelly

The mind of a person plans his way
But the Lord directs his steps

~ Proverbs 16:9

The Wisdom Journal
Monthly Goals

www.wisdomjournal.org

NOTES

Dreams & Goals for My Faith

_____

_____

_____

Dreams & Goals for My Family & Friendships

_____

_____

_____

Dreams & Goals for My Fitness

_____

_____

_____

Dreams & Goals for My Finances

_____

_____

_____

Dreams & Goals for My Career

_____

_____

_____

Dreams & Goals for My Contribution

_____

_____

_____

Wisdom is better than rubies

~Proverbs 8:1

Your Journey Begins

The fear of the Lord is the beginning of wisdom

~ Proverbs 9:10

1 The proverbs of Solomon the son of David, king of Israel:
2 To know wisdom and instruction,
To discern the sayings of understanding,
3 To receive instruction in wise behavior,
Righteousness, justice and equity;
4 To give prudence to the naive,
To the youth knowledge and discretion,
5 A wise man will hear and increase in learning,
And a man of understanding will acquire wise counsel,
6 To understand a proverb and a figure,
The words of the wise and their riddles.
7 The fear of the LORD is the beginning of knowledge;
Fools despise wisdom and instruction.
8 Hear, my son, your father's instruction
And do not forsake your mother's teaching;
9 Indeed, they are a graceful wreath to your head
And ornaments about your neck.
10 My son, if sinners entice you, Do not consent.
11 If they say, "Come with us,
Let us lie in wait for blood,
Let us ambush the innocent without cause;
12 Let us swallow them alive like Sheol,
Even whole, as those who go down to the pit;
13 We will find all *kinds* of precious wealth,
We will fill our houses with spoil;
14 Throw in your lot with us,
We shall all have one purse,"
15 My son, do not walk in the way with them.
Keep your feet from their path,
16 For their feet run to evil
And they hasten to shed blood.
17 Indeed, it is useless to spread the *baited* net
In the sight of any bird;
18 But they lie in wait for their own blood;
They ambush their own lives.

19 So are the ways of everyone who gains by violence;
It takes away the life of its possessors.
20 Wisdom shouts in the street,
She lifts her voice in the square;
21 At the head of the noisy *streets* she cries out;
At the entrance of the gates in the city she utters her sayings:
22 "How long, O naive ones, will you love being simple-minded? And scoffers delight themselves in scoffing
And fools hate knowledge?
23 "Turn to my reproof,
Behold, I will pour out my spirit on you;
I will make my words known to you.
24 "Because I called and you refused,
I stretched out my hand and no one paid attention;
25 And you neglected all my counsel
And did not want my reproof;
26 I will also laugh at your calamity;
I will mock when your dread comes,
27 When your dread comes like a storm
And your calamity comes like a whirlwind,
When distress and anguish come upon you.
28 "Then they will call on me, but I will not answer;
They will seek me diligently but they will not find me,
29 Because they hated knowledge
And did not choose the fear of the LORD.
30 "They would not accept my counsel,
They spurned all my reproof.
31 "So they shall eat of the fruit of their own way
And be satiated with their own devices.
32 "For the waywardness of the naive will kill them,
And the complacency of fools will destroy them.
33 "But he who listens to me shall live securely
And will be at ease from the dread of evil."

NOTES

32

Proverbs 1
~ Day ~

❖ Wisdom for Today

_____

_____

❖ Interpretation for Today

_____

_____

_____

_____

_____

❖ Strategy for Today

_____

_____

_____

_____

_____

Proverbs 1
~ Night ~

❖ Evaluation for Today

_____

_____

_____

_____

_____

_____

_____

_____

1 My son, if you will receive my words
And treasure my commandments within you,
2 Make your ear attentive to wisdom,
Incline your heart to understanding;
3 For if you cry for discernment,
Lift your voice for understanding;
4 If you seek her as silver
And search for her as for hidden treasures;
5 Then you will discern the fear of the LORD
And discover the knowledge of God.
6 For the LORD gives wisdom;
From His mouth *come* knowledge and understanding.
7 He stores up sound wisdom for the upright;
He is a shield to those who walk in integrity,
8 Guarding the paths of justice,
And He preserves the way of His godly ones.
9 Then you will discern righteousness and justice
And equity *and* every good course.
10 For wisdom will enter your heart
And knowledge will be pleasant to your soul;
11 Discretion will guard you,
Understanding will watch over you,
12 To deliver you from the way of evil,
From the man who speaks perverse things;
13 From those who leave the paths of uprightness
To walk in the ways of darkness;
14 Who delight in doing evil
And rejoice in the perversity of evil;
15 Whose paths are crooked,
And who are devious in their ways;
16 To deliver you from the strange woman,
From the adulteress who flatters with her words;
17 That leaves the companion of her youth
And forgets the covenant of her God;

18 For her house sinks down to death
And her tracks *lead* to the dead;
19 None who go to her return again,
Nor do they reach the paths of life.
20 So you will walk in the way of good men
And keep to the paths of the righteous.
21 For the upright will live in the land
And the blameless will remain in it;
22 But the wicked will be cut off from the land
And the treacherous will be uprooted from it

NOTES

Proverbs 2
~ Day ~

❖ Wisdom for Today

_____

_____

❖ Interpretation for Today

_____

_____

_____

_____

_____

❖ Strategy for Today

_____

_____

_____

_____

_____

Proverbs 2
~ Night ~

❖ Evaluation for Today

_____

_____

_____

_____

_____

_____

_____

_____

1 My son, do not forget my teaching,
But let your heart keep my commandments;
2 For length of days and years of life
And peace they will add to you.
3 Do not let kindness and truth leave you;
Bind them around your neck,
Write them on the tablet of your heart.
4 So you will find favor and good repute
In the sight of God and man.
5 Trust in the LORD with all your heart
And do not lean on your own understanding.
6 In all your ways acknowledge Him,
And He will make your paths straight.
7 Do not be wise in your own eyes;
Fear the LORD and turn away from evil.
8 It will be healing to your body
And refreshment to your bones.
9 Honor the LORD from your wealth
And from the first of all your produce;
10 So your barns will be filled with plenty
And your vats will overflow with new wine.
11 My son, do not reject the discipline of the LORD
Or loathe His reproof,
12 For whom the LORD loves He reproves,
Even as a father *corrects* the son in whom he delights.
13 How blessed is the man who finds wisdom
And the man who gains understanding.
14 For her profit is better than the profit of silver
And her gain better than fine gold.
15 She is more precious than jewels;
And nothing you desire compares with her.
16 Long life is in her right hand;
In her left hand are riches and honor.
17 Her ways are pleasant ways
And all her paths are peace.

18 She is a tree of life to those who take hold of her,
And happy are all who hold her fast.
19 The LORD by wisdom founded the earth,
By understanding He established the heavens.
20 By His knowledge the deeps were broken up
And the skies drip with dew.
21 My son, let them not vanish from your sight;
Keep sound wisdom and discretion,
22 So they will be life to your soul
And adornment to your neck.
23 Then you will walk in your way securely
And your foot will not stumble.
24 When you lie down, you will not be afraid;
When you lie down, your sleep will be sweet.
25 Do not be afraid of sudden fear
Nor of the onslaught of the wicked when it comes;
26 For the LORD will be your confidence
And will keep your foot from being caught.
27 Do not withhold good from those to whom it is due,
When it is in your power to do *it*.
28 Do not say to your neighbor, "Go, and come back,
And tomorrow I will give *it*,"
When you have it with you.
29 Do not devise harm against your neighbor,
While he lives securely beside you.
30 Do not contend with a man without cause,
If he has done you no harm.
31 Do not envy a man of violence
And do not choose any of his ways.
32 For the devious are an abomination to the LORD;
But He is intimate with the upright.
33 The curse of the LORD is on the house of the wicked,
But He blesses the dwelling of the righteous.
34 Though He scoffs at the scoffers,
Yet He gives grace to the afflicted.
35 The wise will inherit honor,
But fools display dishonor.

NOTES

Proverbs 3
~ Day ~

❖ Wisdom for Today

_____

_____

❖ Interpretation for Today

_____

_____

_____

_____

_____

❖ Strategy for Today

_____

_____

_____

_____

_____

Proverbs 3
~ Night ~

❖ Evaluation for Today

_____

_____

_____

_____

_____

_____

_____

_____

1 Hear, *O* sons, the instruction of a father,
And give attention that you may gain understanding,
2 For I give you sound teaching;
Do not abandon my instruction.
3 When I was a son to my father,
Tender and the only son in the sight of my mother,
4 Then he taught me and said to me,
"Let your heart hold fast my words;
Keep my commandments and live;
5 Acquire wisdom! Acquire understanding!
Do not forget nor turn away from the words of my mouth.
6 "Do not forsake her, and she will guard you;
Love her, and she will watch over you.
7 "The beginning of wisdom *is:* Acquire wisdom;
And with all your acquiring, get understanding.
8 "Prize her, and she will exalt you;
She will honor you if you embrace her.
9 "She will place on your head a garland of grace;
She will present you with a crown of beauty."
10 Hear, my son, and accept my sayings
And the years of your life will be many.
11 I have directed you in the way of wisdom;
I have led you in upright paths.
12 When you walk, your steps will not be impeded;
And if you run, you will not stumble.
13 Take hold of instruction; do not let go.
Guard her, for she is your life.
14 Do not enter the path of the wicked
And do not proceed in the way of evil men.
15 Avoid it, do not pass by it;
Turn away from it and pass on.
16 For they cannot sleep unless they do evil;
And they are robbed of sleep unless they
make *someone* stumble.

17 For they eat the bread of wickedness
And drink the wine of violence.
18 But the path of the righteous is like the light of dawn,
That shines brighter and brighter until the full day.
19 The way of the wicked is like darkness;
They do not know over what they stumble.
20 My son, give attention to my words;
Incline your ear to my sayings.
21 Do not let them depart from your sight;
Keep them in the midst of your heart.
22 For they are life to those who find them
And health to all their body.
23 Watch over your heart with all diligence,
For from it *flow* the springs of life.
24 Put away from you a deceitful mouth
And put devious speech far from you.
25 Let your eyes look directly ahead
And let your gaze be fixed straight in front of you.
26 Watch the path of your feet
And all your ways will be established.
27 Do not turn to the right nor to the left;
Turn your foot from evil.

NOTES

Proverbs 4
~ Day ~

❖ Wisdom for Today

_____

_____

❖ Interpretation for Today

_____

_____

_____

_____

_____

❖ Strategy for Today

_____

_____

_____

_____

_____

Proverbs 4
~ Night ~

❖ Evaluation for Today

_____

_____

_____

_____

_____

_____

_____

_____

1 My son, give attention to my wisdom,
Incline your ear to my understanding;
2 That you may observe discretion
And your lips may reserve knowledge.
3 For the lips of an adulteress drip honey
And smoother than oil is her speech;
4 But in the end she is bitter as wormwood,
Sharp as a two-edged sword.
5 Her feet go down to death,
Her steps take hold of Sheol.
6 She does not ponder the path of life;
Her ways are unstable, she does not know *it*.
7 Now then, *my* sons, listen to me
And do not depart from the words of my mouth.
8 Keep your way far from her
And do not go near the door of her house,
9 Or you will give your vigor to others
And your years to the cruel one;
10 And strangers will be filled with your strength
And your hard-earned goods *will go* to the house of an alien;
11 And you groan at your final end,
When your flesh and your body are consumed;
12 And you say, "How I have hated instruction!
And my heart spurned reproof!
13 "I have not listened to the voice of my teachers,
Nor inclined my ear to my instructors!
14 "I was almost in utter ruin
In the midst of the assembly and congregation."
15 Drink water from your own cistern
And fresh water from your own well.
16 Should your springs be dispersed abroad,
Streams of water in the streets?
17 Let them be yours alone
And not for strangers with you.

18 Let your fountain be blessed,
And rejoice in the wife of your youth.
19 *As* a loving hind and a graceful doe,
Let her breasts satisfy you at all times;
Be exhilarated always with her love.
20 For why should you, my son, be exhilarated with an
adulteress And embrace the bosom of a foreigner?
21 For the ways of a man are before the eyes of the LORD,
And He watches all his paths.
22 His own iniquities will capture the wicked,
And he will be held with the cords of his sin.
23 He will die for lack of instruction,
And in the greatness of his folly he will go astray.

NOTES

Proverbs 5
~ Day ~

❖ Wisdom for Today

_____

_____

❖ Interpretation for Today

_____

_____

_____

_____

_____

❖ Strategy for Today

_____

_____

_____

_____

_____

Proverbs 5
~ Night ~

❖ Evaluation for Today

_____

_____

_____

_____

_____

_____

_____

_____

_____

1 My son, if you have become surety for your neighbor,
Have given a pledge for a stranger,
2 *If* you have been snared with the words of your mouth,
Have been caught with the words of your mouth,
3 Do this then, my son, and deliver yourself;
Since you have come into the hand of your neighbor,
Go, humble yourself, and importune your neighbor.
4 Give no sleep to your eyes,
Nor slumber to your eyelids;
5 Deliver yourself like a gazelle from *the hunter's* hand
And like a bird from the hand of the fowler.
6 Go to the ant, O sluggard,
Observe her ways and be wise,
7 Which, having no chief, Officer or ruler,
8 Prepares her food in the summer
And gathers her provision in the harvest.
9 How long will you lie down, O sluggard?
When will you arise from your sleep?
10 "A little sleep, a little slumber,
A little folding of the hands to rest"--
11 Your poverty will come in like a vagabond
And your need like an armed man.
12 A worthless person, a wicked man,
Is the one who walks with a perverse mouth,
13 Who winks with his eyes, who signals with his feet,
Who points with his fingers;
14 Who *with* perversity in his heart continually devises evil,
Who spreads strife.
15 Therefore his calamity will come suddenly;
Instantly he will be broken and there will be no healing.
16 There are six things which the LORD hates,
Yes, seven which are an abomination to Him:
17 Haughty eyes, a lying tongue,
And hands that shed innocent blood,
18 A heart that devises wicked plans,
Feet that run rapidly to evil,

19 A false witness *who* utters lies,
And one who spreads strife among brothers.
20 My son, observe the commandment of your father
And do not forsake the teaching of your mother;
21 Bind them continually on your heart;
Tie them around your neck.
22 When you walk about, they will guide you;
When you sleep, they will watch over you;
And when you awake, they will talk to you.
23 For the commandment is a lamp and the teaching is light;
And reproofs for discipline are the way of life
24 To keep you from the evil woman,
From the smooth tongue of the adulteress.
25 Do not desire her beauty in your heart,
Nor let her capture you with her eyelids.
26 For on account of a harlot *one is reduced* to a loaf of bread,
And an adulteress hunts for the precious life.
27 Can a man take fire in his bosom
And his clothes not be burned?
28 Or can a man walk on hot coals
And his feet not be scorched?
29 So is the one who goes in to his neighbor's wife;
Whoever touches her will not go unpunished.
30 Men do not despise a thief if he steals
To satisfy himself when he is hungry;
31 But when he is found, he must repay sevenfold;
He must give all the substance of his house.
32 The one who commits adultery with a woman is lacking
sense; He who would destroy himself does it.
33 Wounds and disgrace he will find,
And his reproach will not be blotted out.
34 For jealousy enrages a man,
And he will not spare in the day of vengeance.
35 He will not accept any ransom,
Nor will he be satisfied though you give many gifts.

NOTES

Proverbs 6
~ Day ~

❖ Wisdom for Today

_____

_____

❖ Interpretation for Today

_____

_____

_____

_____

_____

❖ Strategy for Today

_____

_____

_____

_____

_____

Proverbs 6
~ Night ~

❖ Evaluation for Today

_____

_____

_____

_____

_____

_____

_____

_____

Proverbs 7

1 My son, keep my words
And treasure my commandments within you.
2 Keep my commandments and live,
And my teaching as the apple of your eye.
3 Bind them on your fingers;
Write them on the tablet of your heart.
4 Say to wisdom, "You are my sister,"
And call understanding *your* intimate friend;
5 That they may keep you from an adulteress,
From the foreigner who flatters with her words.
6 For at the window of my house
I looked out through my lattice,
7 And I saw among the naive,
And discerned among the youths
A young man lacking sense,
8 Passing through the street near her corner;
And he takes the way to her house,
9 In the twilight, in the evening,
In the middle of the night and *in* the darkness.
10 And behold, a woman *comes* to meet him,
Dressed as a harlot and cunning of heart.
11 She is boisterous and rebellious,
Her feet do not remain at home;
12 *She is* now in the streets, now in the squares,
And lurks by every corner.
13 So she seizes him and kisses him
And with a brazen face she says to him:
14 "I was due to offer peace offerings;
Today I have paid my vows.
15 "Therefore I have come out to meet you,
To seek your presence earnestly, and I have found you.
16 "I have spread my couch with coverings,
With colored linens of Egypt.
17 "I have sprinkled my bed
With myrrh, aloes and cinnamon.

18 "Come, let us drink our fill of love until morning;
Let us delight ourselves with caresses.
19 "For my husband is not at home,
He has gone on a long journey;
20 He has taken a bag of money with him,
At the full moon he will come home."
21 With her many persuasions she entices him;
With her flattering lips she seduces him.
22 Suddenly he follows her
As an ox goes to the slaughter,
Or as *one in* fetters to the discipline of a fool,
23 Until an arrow pierces through his liver;
As a bird hastens to the snare,
So he does not know that it *will cost him* his life.
24 Now therefore, *my* sons, listen to me,
And pay attention to the words of my mouth.
25 Do not let your heart turn aside to her ways,
Do not stray into her paths.
26 For many are the victims she has cast down,
And numerous are all her slain.
27 Her house is the way to Sheol,
Descending to the chambers of death.

NOTES

Proverbs 7
~ Day ~

❖ Wisdom for Today

_____

_____

❖ Interpretation for Today

_____

_____

_____

_____

_____

❖ Strategy for Today

_____

_____

_____

_____

_____

Proverbs 7
~ Night ~

❖ Evaluation for Today

_____

_____

_____

_____

_____

_____

_____

_____

_____

1 Does not wisdom call,
And understanding lift up her voice?
2 On top of the heights beside the way,
Where the paths meet, she takes her stand;
3 Beside the gates, at the opening to the city,
At the entrance of the doors, she cries out:
4 "To you, O men, I call, And my voice is to the sons of men.
5 "O naive ones, understand prudence;
And, O fools, understand wisdom.
6 "Listen, for I will speak noble things;
And the opening of my lips *will reveal* right things.
7 "For my mouth will utter truth;
And wickedness is an abomination to my lips.
8 "All the utterances of my mouth are in righteousness;
There is nothing crooked or perverted in them.
9 "They are all straightforward to him who understands,
And right to those who find knowledge.
10 "Take my instruction and not silver,
And knowledge rather than choicest gold.
11 "For wisdom is better than jewels;
And all desirable things cannot compare with her.
12 "I, wisdom, dwell with prudence,
And I find knowledge *and* discretion.
13 "The fear of the LORD is to hate evil;
Pride and arrogance and the evil way
And the perverted mouth, I hate.
14 "Counsel is mine and sound wisdom;
I am understanding, power is mine.
15 "By me kings reign, And rulers decree justice.
16 "By me princes rule, and nobles, All who judge rightly.
17 "I love those who love me;
And those who diligently seek me will find me.
18 "Riches and honor are with me,
Enduring wealth and righteousness.
19 "My fruit is better than gold, even pure gold,
And my yield *better* than choicest silver.

20 "I walk in the way of righteousness,
In the midst of the paths of justice,
21 To endow those who love me with wealth,
That I may fill their treasuries.
22 "The LORD possessed me at the beginning of His way,
Before His works of old.
23 "From everlasting I was established,
From the beginning, from the earliest times of the earth.
24 "When there were no depths I was brought forth,
When there were no springs abounding with water.
25 "Before the mountains were settled,
Before the hills I was brought forth;
26 While He had not yet made the earth and the fields,
Nor the first dust of the world.
27 "When He established the heavens, I was there,
When He inscribed a circle on the face of the deep,
28 When He made firm the skies above,
When the springs of the deep became fixed,
29 When He set for the sea its boundary
So that the water would not transgress His command,
When He marked out the foundations of the earth;
30 Then I was beside Him, *as* a master workman;
And I was daily *His* delight,
Rejoicing always before Him,
31 Rejoicing in the world, His earth,
And *having* my delight in the sons of men.
32 "Now therefore, O sons, listen to me,
For blessed are they who keep my ways.
33 "Heed instruction and be wise,
And do not neglect *it*.
34 "Blessed is the man who listens to me,
Watching daily at my gates,
Waiting at my doorposts.
35 "For he who finds me finds life
And obtains favor from the LORD.
36 "But he who sins against me injures himself;
All those who hate me love death.

NOTES

Proverbs 8
~ Day ~

❖ Wisdom for Today

_____
_____

❖ Interpretation for Today

_____
_____
_____
_____
_____

❖ Strategy for Today

_____
_____
_____
_____
_____

Proverbs 8
~ Night ~

❖ Evaluation for Today

_____
_____
_____
_____
_____
_____
_____
_____

Proverbs 9

1 Wisdom has built her house,
She has hewn out her seven pillars;
2 She has prepared her food, she has mixed her wine;
She has also set her table;
3 She has sent out her maidens, she calls
From the tops of the heights of the city:
4 "Whoever is naive, let him turn in here!"
To him who lacks understanding she says,
5 "Come, eat of my food
And drink of the wine I have mixed.
6 "Forsake *your* folly and live,
And proceed in the way of understanding."
7 He who corrects a scoffer gets dishonor for himself,
And he who reproves a wicked man *gets* insults for himself.
8 Do not reprove a scoffer, or he will hate you,
Reprove a wise man and he will love you.
9 Give *instruction* to a wise man and he will be still wiser,
Teach a righteous man and he will increase *his* learning.
10 The fear of the LORD is the beginning of wisdom,
And the knowledge of the Holy One is understanding.
11 For by me your days will be multiplied,
And years of life will be added to you.

12 If you are wise, you are wise for yourself,
And if you scoff, you alone will bear it.
13 The woman of folly is boisterous,
She is naive and knows nothing.
14 She sits at the doorway of her house,
On a seat by the high places of the city,
15 Calling to those who pass by,
Who are making their paths straight:
16 "Whoever is naive, let him turn in here,"
And to him who lacks understanding she says,
17 "Stolen water is sweet;
And bread *eaten* in secret is pleasant."
18 But he does not know that the dead are there,
That her guests are in the depths of Sheol.

NOTES

Proverbs 9
~ Day ~

❖ Wisdom for Today

_____

_____

❖ Interpretation for Today

_____

_____

_____

_____

_____

❖ Strategy for Today

_____

_____

_____

_____

_____

Proverbs 9
~ Night ~

❖ Evaluation for Today

_____

_____

_____

_____

_____

_____

_____

_____

1 The proverbs of Solomon.
A wise son makes a father glad,
But a foolish son is a grief to his mother.
2 Ill-gotten gains do not profit,
But righteousness delivers from death.
3 The LORD will not allow the righteous to hunger,
But He will reject the craving of the wicked.
4 Poor is he who works with a negligent hand,
But the hand of the diligent makes rich.
5 He who gathers in summer is a son who acts wisely,
But he who sleeps in harvest is a son who acts shamefully.
6 Blessings are on the head of the righteous,
But the mouth of the wicked conceals violence.
7 The memory of the righteous is blessed,
But the name of the wicked will rot.
8 The wise of heart will receive commands,
But a babbling fool will be ruined.
9 He who walks in integrity walks securely,
But he who perverts his ways will be found out.
10 He who winks the eye causes trouble,
And a babbling fool will be ruined.
11 The mouth of the righteous is a fountain of life,
But the mouth of the wicked conceals violence.
12 Hatred stirs up strife, But love covers all transgressions.
13 On the lips of the discerning, wisdom is found,
But a rod is for the back of him who lacks understanding.
14 Wise men store up knowledge,
But with the mouth of the foolish, ruin is at hand.
15 The rich man's wealth is his fortress,
The ruin of the poor is their poverty.
16 The wages of the righteous is life,
The income of the wicked, punishment.
17 He is *on* the path of life who heeds instruction,
But he who ignores reproof goes astray.

---

18 He who conceals hatred *has* lying lips,
And he who spreads slander is a fool.
19 When there are many words, transgression is
unavoidable, But he who restrains his lips is wise.
20 The tongue of the righteous is *as* choice silver,
The heart of the wicked is *worth* little.
21 The lips of the righteous feed many,
But fools die for lack of understanding.
22 It is the blessing of the LORD that makes rich,
And He adds no sorrow to it.
23 Doing wickedness is like sport to a fool,
And *so is* wisdom to a man of understanding.
24 What the wicked fears will come upon him,
But the desire of the righteous will be granted.
25 When the whirlwind passes, the wicked is no more,
But the righteous *has* an everlasting foundation.
26 Like vinegar to the teeth and smoke to the eyes,
So is the lazy one to those who send him.
27 The fear of the LORD prolongs life,
But the years of the wicked will be shortened.
28 The hope of the righteous is gladness,
But the expectation of the wicked perishes.
29 The way of the LORD is a stronghold to the upright,
But ruin to the workers of iniquity.
30 The righteous will never be shaken,
But the wicked will not dwell in the land.
31 The mouth of the righteous flows with wisdom,
But the perverted tongue will be cut out.
32 The lips of the righteous bring forth what is acceptable,
But the mouth of the wicked what is perverted.

NOTES

Proverbs 10
~ Day ~

❖ Wisdom for Today

_____

_____

❖ Interpretation for Today

_____

_____

_____

_____

_____

❖ Strategy for Today

_____

_____

_____

_____

Proverbs 10
~ Night ~

❖ Evaluation for Today

_____

_____

_____

_____

_____

_____

_____

_____

1 A false balance is an abomination to the LORD,
But a just weight is His delight.
2 When pride comes, then comes dishonor,
But with the humble is wisdom.
3 The integrity of the upright will guide them,
But the crookedness of the treacherous will destroy them.
4 Riches do not profit in the day of wrath,
But righteousness delivers from death.
5 The righteousness of the blameless will smooth his way,
But the wicked will fall by his own wickedness.
6 The righteousness of the upright will deliver them,
But the treacherous will be caught by *their own* greed.
7 When a wicked man dies, *his* expectation will perish,
And the hope of strong men perishes.
8 The righteous is delivered from trouble,
But the wicked takes his place.
9 With *his* mouth the godless man destroys his neighbor,
But through knowledge the righteous will be delivered.
10 When it goes well with the righteous, the city rejoices,
And when the wicked perish, there is joyful shouting.
11 By the blessing of the upright a city is exalted,
But by the mouth of the wicked it is torn down.
12 He who despises his neighbor lacks sense,
But a man of understanding keeps silent.
13 He who goes about as a talebearer reveals secrets,
But he who is trustworthy conceals a matter.
14 Where there is no guidance the people fall,
But in abundance of counselors there is victory.
15 He who is guarantor for a stranger will surely suffer for
it, But he who hates being a guarantor is secure.
16 A gracious woman attains honor,
And ruthless men attain riches.
17 The merciful man does himself good,
But the cruel man does himself harm.

18 The wicked earns deceptive wages,
But he who sows righteousness *gets* a true reward.
19 He who is steadfast in righteousness *will attain* to life,
And he who pursues evil *will bring about* his own death.
20 The perverse in heart are an abomination to the LORD,
But the blameless in *their* walk are His delight.
21 Assuredly, the evil man will not go unpunished,
But the descendants of the righteous will be delivered.
22 *As* a ring of gold in a swine's snout
So is a beautiful woman who lacks discretion.
23 The desire of the righteous is only good,
But the expectation of the wicked is wrath.
24 There is one who scatters, and *yet* increases all the
more, And there is one who withholds what is justly due, *and
yet it results* only in want.
25 The generous man will be prosperous,
And he who waters will himself be watered.
26 He who withholds grain, the people will curse him,
But blessing will be on the head of him who sells *it*.
27 He who diligently seeks good seeks favor,
But he who seeks evil, evil will come to him.
28 He who trusts in his riches will fall,
But the righteous will flourish like the *green* leaf.
29 He who troubles his own house will inherit wind,
And the foolish will be servant to the wisehearted.
30 The fruit of the righteous is a tree of life,
And he who is wise wins souls.
31 If the righteous will be rewarded in the earth,
How much more the wicked and the sinner!

NOTES

Proverbs 11
~ Day ~

❖ Wisdom for Today

_____

_____

❖ Interpretation for Today

_____

_____

_____

_____

_____

❖ Strategy for Today

_____

_____

_____

_____

_____

Proverbs 11
~ Night ~

❖ Evaluation for Today

_____

_____

_____

_____

_____

_____

_____

_____

1 Whoever loves discipline loves knowledge,
But he who hates reproof is stupid.
2 A good man will obtain favor from the LORD,
But He will condemn a man who devises evil.
3 A man will not be established by wickedness,
But the root of the righteous will not be moved.
4 An excellent wife is the crown of her husband,
But she who shames *him* is like rottenness in his bones.
5 The thoughts of the righteous are just,
But the counsels of the wicked are deceitful.
6 The words of the wicked lie in wait for blood,
But the mouth of the upright will deliver them.
7 The wicked are overthrown and are no more,
But the house of the righteous will stand.
8 A man will be praised according to his insight,
But one of perverse mind will be despised.
9 Better is he who is lightly esteemed and has a servant
Than he who honors himself and lacks bread.
10 A righteous man has regard for the life of his animal,
But *even* the compassion of the wicked is cruel.
11 He who tills his land will have plenty of bread,
But he who pursues worthless *things* lacks sense.
12 The wicked man desires the booty of evil men,
But the root of the righteous yields *fruit.*
13 An evil man is ensnared by the transgression of his lips,
But the righteous will escape from trouble.
14 A man will be satisfied with good by the fruit of his
words, And the deeds of a man's hands will return to him.
15 The way of a fool is right in his own eyes,
But a wise man is he who listens to counsel.
16 A fool's anger is known at once,
But a prudent man conceals dishonor.
17 He who speaks truth tells what is right,
But a false witness, deceit.

---

18 There is one who speaks rashly like the thrusts of a sword, But the tongue of the wise brings healing.
19 Truthful lips will be established forever, But a lying tongue is only for a moment.
20 Deceit is in the heart of those who devise evil, But counselors of peace have joy.
21 No harm befalls the righteous, But the wicked are filled with trouble.
22 Lying lips are an abomination to the LORD, But those who deal faithfully are His delight.
23 A prudent man conceals knowledge, But the heart of fools proclaims folly.
24 The hand of the diligent will rule, But the slack *hand* will be put to forced labor.
25 Anxiety in a man's heart weighs it down, But a good word makes it glad.
26 The righteous is a guide to his neighbor, But the way of the wicked leads them astray.
27 A lazy man does not roast his prey, But the precious possession of a man *is* diligence.
28 In the way of righteousness is life, And in *its* pathway there is no death.

NOTES

Proverbs 12
~ Day ~

❖ Wisdom for Today

_____

_____

❖ Interpretation for Today

_____

_____

_____

_____

_____

❖ Strategy for Today

_____

_____

_____

_____

_____

Proverbs 12
~ Night ~

❖ Evaluation for Today

_____

_____

_____

_____

_____

_____

_____

_____

1 A wise son *accepts his* father's discipline,
But a scoffer does not listen to rebuke.
2 From the fruit of a man's mouth he enjoys good,
But the desire of the treacherous is violence.
3 The one who guards his mouth preserves his life;
The one who opens wide his lips comes to ruin.
4 The soul of the sluggard craves and *gets* nothing,
But the soul of the diligent is made fat.
5 A righteous man hates falsehood,
But a wicked man acts disgustingly and shamefully.
6 Righteousness guards the one whose way is blameless,
But wickedness subverts the sinner.
7 There is one who pretends to be rich, but has nothing;
Another pretends to be poor, but has great wealth.
8 The ransom of a man's life is his wealth,
But the poor hears no rebuke.
9 The light of the righteous rejoices,
But the lamp of the wicked goes out.
10 Through insolence comes nothing but strife,
But wisdom is with those who receive counsel.
11 Wealth *obtained* by fraud dwindles,
But the one who gathers by labor increases *it.*
12 Hope deferred makes the heart sick,
But desire fulfilled is a tree of life.
13 The one who despises the word will be in debt to it,
But the one who fears the commandment will be rewarded.
14 The teaching of the wise is a fountain of life,
To turn aside from the snares of death.
15 Good understanding produces favor,
But the way of the treacherous is hard.
16 Every prudent man acts with knowledge,
But a fool displays folly.
17 A wicked messenger falls into adversity,
But a faithful envoy *brings* healing.

18 Poverty and shame *will come* to him who neglects discipline, But he who regards reproof will be honored.
19 Desire realized is sweet to the soul,
But it is an abomination to fools to turn away from evil.
20 He who walks with wise men will be wise,
But the companion of fools will suffer harm.
21 Adversity pursues sinners,
But the righteous will be rewarded with prosperity.
22 A good man leaves an inheritance to his children's children, And the wealth of the sinner is stored up for the righteous.
23 Abundant food *is in* the fallow ground of the poor,
But it is swept away by injustice.
24 He who withholds his rod hates his son,
But he who loves him disciplines him diligently.
25 The righteous has enough to satisfy his appetite,
But the stomach of the wicked is in need.

NOTES

Proverbs 13
~ Day ~

❖ Wisdom for Today

_____
_____

❖ Interpretation for Today

_____
_____
_____
_____
_____

❖ Strategy for Today

_____
_____
_____
_____
_____

Proverbs 13
~ Night ~

❖ Evaluation for Today

_____
_____
_____
_____
_____
_____
_____
_____

81

Proverbs 14

1 The wise woman builds her house,
But the foolish tears it down with her own hands.
2 He who walks in his uprightness fears the LORD,
But he who is devious in his ways despises Him.
3 In the mouth of the foolish is a rod for *his* back,
But the lips of the wise will protect them.
4 Where no oxen are, the manger is clean,
But much revenue *comes* by the strength of the ox.
5 A trustworthy witness will not lie,
But a false witness utters lies.
6 A scoffer seeks wisdom and *finds* none,
But knowledge is easy to one who has understanding.
7 Leave the presence of a fool,
Or you will not discern words of knowledge.
8 The wisdom of the sensible is to understand his way,
But the foolishness of fools is deceit.
9 Fools mock at sin,
But among the upright there is good will.
10 The heart knows its own bitterness,
And a stranger does not share its joy.
11 The house of the wicked will be destroyed,
But the tent of the upright will flourish.
12 There is a way *which seems* right to a man,
But its end is the way of death.
13 Even in laughter the heart may be in pain,
And the end of joy may be grief.
14 The backslider in heart will have his fill of his own
ways, But a good man will *be satisfied* with his.
15 The naive believes everything,
But the sensible man considers his steps.
16 A wise man is cautious and turns away from evil,
But a fool is arrogant and careless.
17 A quick-tempered man acts foolishly,
And a man of evil devices is hated.

---

18 The naive inherit foolishness,
But the sensible are crowned with knowledge.
19 The evil will bow down before the good,
And the wicked at the gates of the righteous.
20 The poor is hated even by his neighbor,
But those who love the rich are many.
21 He who despises his neighbor sins,
But happy is he who is gracious to the poor.
22 Will they not go astray who devise evil?
But kindness and truth *will be to* those who devise good.
23 In all labor there is profit,
But mere talk *leads* only to poverty.
24 The crown of the wise is their riches,
But the folly of fools is foolishness.
25 A truthful witness saves lives,
But he who utters lies is treacherous.
26 In the fear of the LORD there is strong confidence,
And his children will have refuge.
27 The fear of the LORD is a fountain of life,
That one may avoid the snares of death.
28 In a multitude of people is a king's glory,
But in the dearth of people is a prince's ruin.
29 He who is slow to anger has great understanding,
But he who is quick-tempered exalts folly.
30 A tranquil heart is life to the body,
But passion is rottenness to the bones.
31 He who oppresses the poor taunts his Maker,
But he who is gracious to the needy honors Him.
32 The wicked is thrust down by his wrongdoing,
But the righteous has a refuge when he dies.
33 Wisdom rests in the heart of one who has
understanding, But in the hearts of fools it is made known.
34 Righteousness exalts a nation,
But sin is a disgrace to *any* people.
35 The king's favor is toward a servant who acts wisely,
But his anger is toward him who acts shamefully.

NOTES

Proverbs 14
~ Day ~

❖ Wisdom for Today

_____

_____

❖ Interpretation for Today

_____

_____

_____

_____

_____

❖ Strategy for Today

_____

_____

_____

_____

_____

Proverbs 14
~ Night ~

❖ Evaluation for Today

_____

_____

_____

_____

_____

_____

_____

_____

1 A gentle answer turns away wrath,
But a harsh word stirs up anger.
2 The tongue of the wise makes knowledge acceptable,
But the mouth of fools spouts folly.
3 The eyes of the LORD are in every place,
Watching the evil and the good.
4 A soothing tongue is a tree of life,
But perversion in it crushes the spirit.
5 A fool rejects his father's discipline,
But he who regards reproof is sensible.
6 Great wealth is *in* the house of the righteous,
But trouble is in the income of the wicked.
7 The lips of the wise spread knowledge,
But the hearts of fools are not so.
8 The sacrifice of the wicked is an abomination to the LORD,
But the prayer of the upright is His delight.
9 The way of the wicked is an abomination to the LORD,
But He loves one who pursues righteousness.
10 Grievous punishment is for him who forsakes the way;
He who hates reproof will die.
11 Sheol and Abaddon *lie open* before the LORD,
How much more the hearts of men!
12 A scoffer does not love one who reproves him,
He will not go to the wise.
13 A joyful heart makes a cheerful face,
But when the heart is sad, the spirit is broken.
14 The mind of the intelligent seeks knowledge,
But the mouth of fools feeds on folly.
15 All the days of the afflicted are bad,
But a cheerful heart *has* a continual feast.
16 Better is a little with the fear of the LORD
Than great treasure and turmoil with it.
17 Better is a dish of vegetables where love is
Than a fattened ox *served* with hatred.

18 A hot-tempered man stirs up strife,
But the slow to anger calms a dispute.
19 The way of the lazy is as a hedge of thorns,
But the path of the upright is a highway.
20 A wise son makes a father glad,
But a foolish man despises his mother.
21 Folly is joy to him who lacks sense,
But a man of understanding walks straight.
22 Without consultation, plans are frustrated,
But with many counselors they succeed.
23 A man has joy in an apt answer,
And how delightful is a timely word!
24 The path of life *leads* upward for the wise
That he may keep away from Sheol below.
25 The LORD will tear down the house of the proud,
But He will establish the boundary of the widow.
26 Evil plans are an abomination to the LORD,
But pleasant words are pure.
27 He who profits illicitly troubles his own house,
But he who hates bribes will live.
28 The heart of the righteous ponders how to answer,
But the mouth of the wicked pours out evil things.
29 The LORD is far from the wicked,
But He hears the prayer of the righteous.
30 Bright eyes gladden the heart;
Good news puts fat on the bones.
31 He whose ear listens to the life-giving reproof
Will dwell among the wise.
32 He who neglects discipline despises himself,
But he who listens to reproof acquires understanding.
33 The fear of the LORD is the instruction for wisdom,
And before honor *comes* humility.

NOTES

Proverbs 15
~ Day ~

❖ Wisdom for Today

_____

_____

❖ Interpretation for Today

_____

_____

_____

_____

_____

❖ Strategy for Today

_____

_____

_____

_____

_____

Proverbs 15
~ Night ~

❖ Evaluation for Today

_____

_____

_____

_____

_____

_____

_____

_____

1 The plans of the heart belong to man,
But the answer of the tongue is from the LORD.
2 All the ways of a man are clean in his own sight,
But the LORD weighs the motives.
3 Commit your works to the LORD
And your plans will be established.
4 The LORD has made everything for its own purpose,
Even the wicked for the day of evil.
5 Everyone who is proud in heart is an abomination to the
LORD; Assuredly, he will not be unpunished.
6 By lovingkindness and truth iniquity is atoned for,
And by the fear of the LORD one keeps away from evil.
7 When a man's ways are pleasing to the LORD,
He makes even his enemies to be at peace with him.
8 Better is a little with righteousness
Than great income with injustice.
9 The mind of man plans his way,
But the LORD directs his steps.
10 A divine decision is in the lips of the king;
His mouth should not err in judgment.
11 A just balance and scales belong to the LORD;
All the weights of the bag are His concern.
12 It is an abomination for kings to commit wicked acts,
For a throne is established on righteousness.
13 Righteous lips are the delight of kings,
And he who speaks right is loved.
14 The fury of a king is *like* messengers of death,
But a wise man will appease it.
15 In the light of a king's face is life,
And his favor is like a cloud with the spring rain.
16 How much better it is to get wisdom than gold!
And to get understanding is to be chosen above silver.
17 The highway of the upright is to depart from evil;
He who watches his way preserves his life.

---

18 Pride *goes* before destruction,
And a haughty spirit before stumbling.
19 It is better to be humble in spirit with the lowly
Than to divide the spoil with the proud.
20 He who gives attention to the word will find good,
And blessed is he who trusts in the LORD.
21 The wise in heart will be called understanding,
And sweetness of speech increases persuasiveness.
22 Understanding is a fountain of life to one who has it,
But the discipline of fools is folly.
23 The heart of the wise instructs his mouth
And adds persuasiveness to his lips.
24 Pleasant words are a honeycomb,
Sweet to the soul and healing to the bones.
25 There is a way *which seems* right to a man,
But its end is the way of death.
26 A worker's appetite works for him,
For his hunger urges him *on.*
27 A worthless man digs up evil,
While his words are like scorching fire.
28 A perverse man spreads strife,
And a slanderer separates intimate friends.
29 A man of violence entices his neighbor
And leads him in a way that is not good.
30 He who winks his eyes *does so* to devise perverse things; He
who compresses his lips brings evil to pass.
31 A gray head is a crown of glory;
It is found in the way of righteousness.
32 He who is slow to anger is better than the mighty,
And he who rules his spirit, than he who captures a city.
33 The lot is cast into the lap,
But its every decision is from the LORD.

NOTES

Proverbs 16
~ Day ~

❖ Wisdom for Today

_____

_____

❖ Interpretation for Today

_____

_____

_____

_____

_____

❖ Strategy for Today

_____

_____

_____

_____

_____

Proverbs 16
~ Night ~

❖ Evaluation for Today

_____

_____

_____

_____

_____

_____

_____

_____

Proverbs 17

1 Better is a dry morsel and quietness with it
Than a house full of feasting with strife.
2 A servant who acts wisely will rule over a son who acts
shamefully,
And will share in the inheritance among brothers.
3 The refining pot is for silver and the furnace for gold,
But the LORD tests hearts.
4 An evildoer listens to wicked lips;
A liar pays attention to a destructive tongue.
5 He who mocks the poor taunts his Maker;
He who rejoices at calamity will not go unpunished.
6 Grandchildren are the crown of old men,
And the glory of sons is their fathers.
7 Excellent speech is not fitting for a fool,
Much less are lying lips to a prince.
8 A bribe is a charm in the sight of its owner;
Wherever he turns, he prospers.
9 He who conceals a transgression seeks love,
But he who repeats a matter separates intimate friends.
10 A rebuke goes deeper into one who has understanding
Than a hundred blows into a fool.
11 A rebellious man seeks only evil,
So a cruel messenger will be sent against him.
12 Let a man meet a bear robbed of her cubs,
Rather than a fool in his folly.
13 He who returns evil for good,
Evil will not depart from his house.
14 The beginning of strife is *like* letting out water,
So abandon the quarrel before it breaks out.
15 He who justifies the wicked and he who condemns the
righteous, Both of them alike are an abomination to the
LORD.
16 Why is there a price in the hand of a fool to buy
wisdom, When he has no sense?

17 A friend loves at all times,
And a brother is born for adversity.
18 A man lacking in sense pledges
And becomes guarantor in the presence of his neighbor.
19 He who loves transgression loves strife;
He who raises his door seeks destruction.
20 He who has a crooked mind finds no good,
And he who is perverted in his language falls into evil.
21 He who sires a fool *does so* to his sorrow,
And the father of a fool has no joy.
22 A joyful heart is good medicine,
But a broken spirit dries up the bones.
23 A wicked man receives a bribe from the bosom
To pervert the ways of justice.
24 Wisdom is in the presence of the one who has understanding,
But the eyes of a fool are on the ends of the earth.
25 A foolish son is a grief to his father
And bitterness to her who bore him.
26 It is also not good to fine the righteous,
Nor to strike the noble for *their* uprightness.
27 He who restrains his words has knowledge,
And he who has a cool spirit is a man of understanding.
28 Even a fool, when he keeps silent, is considered wise;
When he closes his lips, he is *considered* prudent.

NOTES

Proverbs 17
~ Day ~

❖ Wisdom for Today

_____

_____

❖ Interpretation for Today

_____

_____

_____

_____

_____

❖ Strategy for Today

_____

_____

_____

_____

Proverbs 17
~ Night ~

❖ Evaluation for Today

_____

_____

_____

_____

_____

_____

_____

1 He who separates himself seeks *his own* desire,
He quarrels against all sound wisdom.
2 A fool does not delight in understanding,
But only in revealing his own mind.
3 When a wicked man comes, contempt also comes,
And with dishonor *comes* scorn.
4 The words of a man's mouth are deep waters;
The fountain of wisdom is a bubbling brook.
5 To show partiality to the wicked is not good,
Nor to thrust aside the righteous in judgment.
6 A fool's lips bring strife,
And his mouth calls for blows.
7 A fool's mouth is his ruin,
And his lips are the snare of his soul.
8 The words of a whisperer are like dainty morsels,
And they go down into the innermost parts of the body.
9 He also who is slack in his work
Is brother to him who destroys.
10 The name of the LORD is a strong tower;
The righteous runs into it and is safe.
11 A rich man's wealth is his strong city,
And like a high wall in his own imagination.
12 Before destruction the heart of man is haughty,
But humility *goes* before honor.
13 He who gives an answer before he hears,
It is folly and shame to him.
14 The spirit of a man can endure his sickness,
But *as for* a broken spirit who can bear it?
15 The mind of the prudent acquires knowledge,
And the ear of the wise seeks knowledge.
16 A man's gift makes room for him
And brings him before great men.
17 The first to plead his case *seems* right,
Until another comes and examines him.

18 The *cast* lot puts an end to strife
And decides between the mighty ones.
19 A brother offended *is harder to be won* than a strong
city, And contentions are like the bars of a citadel.
20 With the fruit of a man's mouth his stomach will be
satisfied; He will be satisfied *with* the product of his lips.
21 Death and life are in the power of the tongue,
And those who love it will eat its fruit.
22 He who finds a wife finds a good thing
And obtains favor from the LORD.
23 The poor man utters supplications,
But the rich man answers roughly.
24 A man of *too many* friends *comes* to ruin,
But there is a friend who sticks closer than a brother.

NOTES

Proverbs 18
~ Day ~

❖ Wisdom for Today

_____

_____

❖ Interpretation for Today

_____

_____

_____

_____

_____

❖ Strategy for Today

_____

_____

_____

_____

_____

Proverbs 18
~ Night ~

❖ Evaluation for Today

_____

_____

_____

_____

_____

_____

_____

_____

Better is a poor man who walks in his integrity
Than he who is perverse in speech and is a fool.
2 Also it is not good for a person to be without knowledge,
And he who hurries his footsteps errs.
3 The foolishness of man ruins his way,
And his heart rages against the LORD.
4 Wealth adds many friends,
But a poor man is separated from his friend.
5 A false witness will not go unpunished,
And he who tells lies will not escape.
6 Many will seek the favor of a generous man,
And every man is a friend to him who gives gifts.
7 All the brothers of a poor man hate him;
How much more do his friends abandon him!
He pursues *them with* words, *but* they are gone.
8 He who gets wisdom loves his own soul;
He who keeps understanding will find good.
9 A false witness will not go unpunished,
And he who tells lies will perish.
10 Luxury is not fitting for a fool;
Much less for a slave to rule over princes.
11 A man's discretion makes him slow to anger,
And it is his glory to overlook a transgression.
12 The king's wrath is like the roaring of a lion,
But his favor is like dew on the grass.
13 A foolish son is destruction to his father,
And the contentions of a wife are a constant dripping.
14 House and wealth are an inheritance from fathers,
But a prudent wife is from the LORD.
15 Laziness casts into a deep sleep,
And an idle man will suffer hunger.
16 He who keeps the commandment keeps his soul,
But he who is careless of conduct will die.
17 One who is gracious to a poor man lends to the LORD,
And He will repay him for his good deed.

18 Discipline your son while there is hope,
And do not desire his death.
19 *A man of* great anger will bear the penalty,
For if you rescue *him,* you will only have to do it again.
20 Listen to counsel and accept discipline,
That you may be wise the rest of your days.
21 Many plans are in a man's heart,
But the counsel of the LORD will stand.
22 What is desirable in a man is his kindness,
And *it is* better to be a poor man than a liar.
23 The fear of the LORD *leads* to life,
So that one may sleep satisfied, untouched by evil.
24 The sluggard buries his hand in the dish,
But will not even bring it back to his mouth.
25 Strike a scoffer and the naive may become shrewd,
But reprove one who has understanding and he will gain knowledge.
26 He who assaults *his* father *and* drives *his* mother away
Is a shameful and disgraceful son.
27 Cease listening, my son, to discipline,
And you will stray from the words of knowledge.
28 A rascally witness makes a mockery of justice,
And the mouth of the wicked spreads iniquity.
29 Judgments are prepared for scoffers,
And blows for the back of fools.

NOTES

Proverbs 19
~ Day ~

❖ Wisdom for Today

_____

_____

❖ Interpretation for Today

_____

_____

_____

_____

_____

❖ Strategy for Today

_____

_____

_____

_____

_____

Proverbs 19
~ Night ~

❖ Evaluation for Today

_____

_____

_____

_____

_____

_____

_____

_____

1 Wine is a mocker, strong drink a brawler,
And whoever is intoxicated by it is not wise.
2 The terror of a king is like the growling of a lion;
He who provokes him to anger forfeits his own life.
3 Keeping away from strife is an honor for a man,
But any fool will quarrel.
4 The sluggard does not plow after the autumn,
So he begs during the harvest and has nothing.
5 A plan in the heart of a man is *like* deep water,
But a man of understanding draws it out.
6 Many a man proclaims his own loyalty,
But who can find a trustworthy man?
7 A righteous man who walks in his integrity--
How blessed are his sons after him.
8 A king who sits on the throne of justice
Disperses all evil with his eyes.
9 Who can say, "I have cleansed my heart,
I am pure from my sin"?
10 Differing weights and differing measures,
Both of them are abominable to the LORD.
11 It is by his deeds that a lad distinguishes himself
If his conduct is pure and right.
12 The hearing ear and the seeing eye,
The LORD has made both of them.
13 Do not love sleep, or you will become poor;
Open your eyes, *and* you will be satisfied with food.
14 "Bad, bad," says the buyer,
But when he goes his way, then he boasts.
15 There is gold, and an abundance of jewels;
But the lips of knowledge are a more precious thing.
16 Take his garment when he becomes surety for a
stranger; And for foreigners, hold him in pledge.
17 Bread obtained by falsehood is sweet to a man,
But afterward his mouth will be filled with gravel.

18 Prepare plans by consultation,
And make war by wise guidance.
19 He who goes about as a slanderer reveals secrets,
Therefore do not associate with a gossip.
20 He who curses his father or his mother,
His lamp will go out in time of darkness.
21 An inheritance gained hurriedly at the beginning
Will not be blessed in the end.
22 Do not say, "I will repay evil";
Wait for the LORD, and He will save you.
23 Differing weights are an abomination to the LORD,
And a false scale is not good.
24 Man's steps are *ordained* by the LORD,
How then can man understand his way?
25 It is a trap for a man to say rashly, "It is holy!"
And after the vows to make inquiry.
26 A wise king winnows the wicked,
And drives the *threshing* wheel over them.
27 The spirit of man is the lamp of the LORD,
Searching all the innermost parts of his being.
28 Loyalty and truth preserve the king,
And he upholds his throne by righteousness.
29 The glory of young men is their strength,
And the honor of old men is their gray hair.
30 Stripes that wound scour away evil,
And strokes *reach* the innermost parts.

NOTES

Proverbs 20
~ Day ~

❖ Wisdom for Today

_____

_____

❖ Interpretation for Today

_____

_____

_____

_____

_____

❖ Strategy for Today

_____

_____

_____

_____

_____

Proverbs 20
~ Night ~

❖ Evaluation for Today

_____

_____

_____

_____

_____

_____

_____

_____

_____

[1] The king's heart is *like* channels of water in the hand of the LORD; He turns it wherever He wishes.

2 Every man's way is right in his own eyes,
But the LORD weighs the hearts.

3 To do righteousness and justice
Is desired by the LORD more than sacrifice.

4 Haughty eyes and a proud heart,
The lamp of the wicked, is sin.

5 The plans of the diligent *lead* surely to advantage,
But everyone who is hasty *comes* surely to poverty.

6 The acquisition of treasures by a lying tongue
Is a fleeting vapor, the pursuit of death.

7 The violence of the wicked will drag them away,
Because they refuse to act with justice.

8 The way of a guilty man is crooked,
But as for the pure, his conduct is upright.

9 It is better to live in a corner of a roof
Than in a house shared with a contentious woman.

10 The soul of the wicked desires evil;
His neighbor finds no favor in his eyes.

11 When the scoffer is punished, the naive becomes wise;
But when the wise is instructed, he receives knowledge.

12 The righteous one considers the house of the wicked,
Turning the wicked to ruin.

13 He who shuts his ear to the cry of the poor
Will also cry himself and not be answered.

14 A gift in secret subdues anger,
And a bribe in the bosom, strong wrath.

15 The exercise of justice is joy for the righteous,
But is terror to the workers of iniquity.

16 A man who wanders from the way of understanding
Will rest in the assembly of the dead.

17 He who loves pleasure *will become* a poor man;
He who loves wine and oil will not become rich.

18 The wicked is a ransom for the righteous,
And the treacherous is in the place of the upright.
19 It is better to live in a desert land
Than with a contentious and vexing woman.
20 There is precious treasure and oil in the dwelling of the
wise, But a foolish man swallows it up.
21 He who pursues righteousness and loyalty
Finds life, righteousness and honor.
22 A wise man scales the city of the mighty
And brings down the stronghold in which they trust.
23 He who guards his mouth and his tongue,
Guards his soul from troubles.
24 "Proud," "Haughty," "Scoffer," are his names,
Who acts with insolent pride.
25 The desire of the sluggard puts him to death,
For his hands refuse to work;
26 All day long he is craving,
While the righteous gives and does not hold back.
27 The sacrifice of the wicked is an abomination,
How much more when he brings it with evil intent!
28 A false witness will perish,
But the man who listens *to the truth* will speak forever.
29 A wicked man displays a bold face,
But as for the upright, he makes his way sure.
30 There is no wisdom and no understanding
And no counsel against the LORD.
31 The horse is prepared for the day of battle,
But victory belongs to the LORD.

NOTES

Proverbs 21
~ Day ~

❖ Wisdom for Today

_____

_____

❖ Interpretation for Today

_____

_____

_____

_____

_____

❖ Strategy for Today

_____

_____

_____

_____

_____

Proverbs 21
~ Night ~

❖ Evaluation for Today

_____

_____

_____

_____

_____

_____

_____

Proverbs 22

1 A *good* name is to be more desired than great wealth,
Favor is better than silver and gold.
2 The rich and the poor have a common bond,
The LORD is the maker of them all.
3 The prudent sees the evil and hides himself,
But the naive go on, and are punished for it.
4 The reward of humility *and* the fear of the LORD
Are riches, honor and life.
5 Thorns *and* snares are in the way of the perverse;
He who guards himself will be far from them.
6 Train up a child in the way he should go,
Even when he is old he will not depart from it.
7 The rich rules over the poor,
And the borrower *becomes* the lender's slave.
8 He who sows iniquity will reap vanity,
And the rod of his fury will perish.
9 He who is generous will be blessed,
For he gives some of his food to the poor.
10 Drive out the scoffer, and contention will go out,
Even strife and dishonor will cease.
11 He who loves purity of heart
And whose speech is gracious, the king is his friend.
12 The eyes of the LORD preserve knowledge,
But He overthrows the words of the treacherous man.
13 The sluggard says, "There is a lion outside;
I will be killed in the streets!"
14 The mouth of an adulteress is a deep pit;
He who is cursed of the LORD will fall into it.
15 Foolishness is bound up in the heart of a child;
The rod of discipline will remove it far from him.
16 He who oppresses the poor to make more for himself
Or who gives to the rich, *will* only *come to* poverty.
17 Incline your ear and hear the words of the wise,
And apply your mind to my knowledge;

18 For it will be pleasant if you keep them within you,
That they may be ready on your lips.
19 So that your trust may be in the LORD,
I have taught you today, even you.
20 Have I not written to you excellent things
Of counsels and knowledge,
21 To make you know the certainty of the words of truth
That you may correctly answer him who sent you?
22 Do not rob the poor because he is poor,
Or crush the afflicted at the gate;
23 For the LORD will plead their case
And take the life of those who rob them.
24 Do not associate with a man *given* to anger;
Or go with a hot-tempered man,
25 Or you will learn his ways
And find a snare for yourself.
26 Do not be among those who give pledges,
Among those who become guarantors for debts.
27 If you have nothing with which to pay,
Why should he take your bed from under you?
28 Do not move the ancient boundary
Which your fathers have set.
29 Do you see a man skilled in his work?
He will stand before kings;
He will not stand before obscure men.

NOTES

Proverbs 22
~ Day ~

❖ Wisdom for Today

_____

_____

❖ Interpretation for Today

_____

_____

_____

_____

_____

❖ Strategy for Today

_____

_____

_____

_____

Proverbs 22
~ Night ~

❖ Evaluation for Today

_____

_____

_____

_____

_____

_____

_____

1 When you sit down to dine with a ruler,
Consider carefully what is before you,
2 And put a knife to your throat
If you are a man of *great* appetite.
3 Do not desire his delicacies, For it is deceptive food.
4 Do not weary yourself to gain wealth,
Cease from your consideration *of it.*
5 When you set your eyes on it, it is gone.
For *wealth* certainly makes itself wings
Like an eagle that flies *toward* the heavens.
6 Do not eat the bread of a selfish man,
Or desire his delicacies;
7 For as he thinks within himself, so he is.
He says to you, "Eat and drink!" But his heart is not with you.
8 You will vomit up the morsel you have eaten,
And waste your compliments.
9 Do not speak in the hearing of a fool,
For he will despise the wisdom of your words.
10 Do not move the ancient boundary
Or go into the fields of the fatherless,
11 For their Redeemer is strong;
He will plead their case against you.
12 Apply your heart to discipline
And your ears to words of knowledge.
13 Do not hold back discipline from the child,
Although you strike him with the rod, he will not die.
14 You shall strike him with the rod
And rescue his soul from Sheol.
15 My son, if your heart is wise, My own heart also will be glad;
16 And my inmost being will rejoice
When your lips speak what is right.
17 Do not let your heart envy sinners,
But *live* in the fear of the LORD always.
18 Surely there is a future, And your hope will not be cut off.
19 Listen, my son, and be wise, And direct your heart in the way.

20 Do not be with heavy drinkers of wine,
Or with gluttonous eaters of meat;
21 For the heavy drinker and the glutton will come to poverty,
And drowsiness will clothe *one* with rags.
22 Listen to your father who begot you,
And do not despise your mother when she is old.
23 Buy truth, and do not sell *it,*
Get wisdom and instruction and understanding.
24 The father of the righteous will greatly rejoice,
And he who sires a wise son will be glad in him.
25 Let your father and your mother be glad,
And let her rejoice who gave birth to you.
26 Give me your heart, my son,
And let your eyes delight in my ways.
27 For a harlot is a deep pit
And an adulterous woman is a narrow well.
28 Surely she lurks as a robber,
And increases the faithless among men.
29 Who has woe? Who has sorrow?
Who has contentions? Who has complaining?
Who has wounds without cause?
Who has redness of eyes?
30 Those who linger long over wine,
Those who go to taste mixed wine.
31 Do not look on the wine when it is red,
When it sparkles in the cup, When it goes down smoothly;
32 At the last it bites like a serpent
And stings like a viper.
33 Your eyes will see strange things
And your mind will utter perverse things.
34 And you will be like one who lies down in the middle of the
sea, Or like one who lies down on the top of a mast.
35 "They struck me, *but* I did not become ill;
They beat me, *but* I did not know *it.*
When shall I awake? I will seek another drink."

NOTES

Proverbs 23
~ Day ~

❖ Wisdom for Today

_____

_____

❖ Interpretation for Today

_____

_____

_____

_____

_____

❖ Strategy for Today

_____

_____

_____

_____

_____

Proverbs 23
~ Night ~

❖ Evaluation for Today

_____

_____

_____

_____

_____

_____

_____

_____

Proverbs 24

Do not be envious of evil men,
Nor desire to be with them;
2 For their minds devise violence,
And their lips talk of trouble.
3 By wisdom a house is built,
And by understanding it is established;
4 And by knowledge the rooms are filled
With all precious and pleasant riches.
5 A wise man is strong,
And a man of knowledge increases power.
6 For by wise guidance you will wage war,
And in abundance of counselors there is victory.
7 Wisdom is *too* exalted for a fool,
He does not open his mouth in the gate.
8 One who plans to do evil,
Men will call a schemer.
9 The devising of folly is sin,
And the scoffer is an abomination to men.
10 If you are slack in the day of distress,
Your strength is limited.
11 Deliver those who are being taken away to death,
And those who are staggering to slaughter, Oh hold *them* back.
12 If you say, "See, we did not know this,"
Does He not consider *it* who weighs the hearts?
And does He not know *it* who keeps your soul?
And will He not render to man according to his work?
13 My son, eat honey, for it is good,
Yes, the honey from the comb is sweet to your taste;
14 Know *that* wisdom is thus for your soul;
If you find *it,* then there will be a future,
And your hope will not be cut off.
15 Do not lie in wait, O wicked man, against the dwelling of the
righteous; Do not destroy his resting place;
16 For a righteous man falls seven times, and rises again,
But the wicked stumble in *time of* calamity.

17 Do not rejoice when your enemy falls,
And do not let your heart be glad when he stumbles;
18 Or the LORD will see *it* and be displeased,
And turn His anger away from him.
19 Do not fret because of evildoers Or be envious of the wicked;
20 For there will be no future for the evil man;
The lamp of the wicked will be put out.
21 My son, fear the LORD and the king;
Do not associate with those who are given to change,
22 For their calamity will rise suddenly,
And who knows the ruin *that comes* from both of them?
23 These also are sayings of the wise.
To show partiality in judgment is not good.
24 He who says to the wicked, "You are righteous,"
Peoples will curse him, nations will abhor him;
25 But to those who rebuke the *wicked* will be delight,
And a good blessing will come upon them.
26 He kisses the lips Who gives a right answer.
27 Prepare your work outside
And make it ready for yourself in the field;
Afterwards, then, build your house.
28 Do not be a witness against your neighbor without cause,
And do not deceive with your lips.
29 Do not say, "Thus I shall do to him as he has done to me;
I will render to the man according to his work."
30 I passed by the field of the sluggard
And by the vineyard of the man lacking sense,
31 And behold, it was completely overgrown with thistles;
Its surface was covered with nettles,
And its stone wall was broken down.
32 When I saw, I reflected upon it;
I looked, *and* received instruction.
33 "A little sleep, a little slumber,
A little folding of the hands to rest,"
34 Then your poverty will come *as* a robber
And your want like an armed man.

NOTES

Proverbs 24
~ Day ~

❖ Wisdom for Today

_____
_____

❖ Interpretation for Today

_____
_____
_____
_____
_____

❖ Strategy for Today

_____
_____
_____
_____
_____

Proverbs 24
~ Night ~

❖ Evaluation for Today

_____
_____
_____
_____
_____
_____
_____

Proverbs 25

1 These also are proverbs of Solomon which the men of
Hezekiah, king of Judah, transcribed.
2 It is the glory of God to conceal a matter,
But the glory of kings is to search out a matter.
3 *As* the heavens for height and the earth for depth,
So the heart of kings is unsearchable.
4 Take away the dross from the silver,
And there comes out a vessel for the smith;
5 Take away the wicked before the king,
And his throne will be established in righteousness.
6 Do not claim honor in the presence of the king,
And do not stand in the place of great men;
7 For it is better that it be said to you, "Come up here,"
Than for you to be placed lower in the presence of the
prince, Whom your eyes have seen.
8 Do not go out hastily to argue *your case;*
Otherwise, what will you do in the end,
When your neighbor humiliates you?
9 Argue your case with your neighbor,
And do not reveal the secret of another,
10 Or he who hears *it* will reproach you,
And the evil report about you will not pass away.
11 *Like* apples of gold in settings of silver
Is a word spoken in right circumstances.
12 *Like* an earring of gold and an ornament of fine gold
Is a wise reprover to a listening ear.
13 Like the cold of snow in the time of harvest
Is a faithful messenger to those who send him,
For he refreshes the soul of his masters.
14 *Like* clouds and wind without rain
Is a man who boasts of his gifts falsely.
15 By forbearance a ruler may be persuaded,
And a soft tongue breaks the bone.
16 Have you found honey? Eat *only* what you need,
That you not have it in excess and vomit it.

17 Let your foot rarely be in your neighbor's house,
Or he will become weary of you and hate you.
18 *Like* a club and a sword and a sharp arrow
Is a man who bears false witness against his neighbor.
19 *Like* a bad tooth and an unsteady foot
Is confidence in a faithless man in time of trouble.
20 *Like* one who takes off a garment on a cold day, *or
like* vinegar on soda,
Is he who sings songs to a troubled heart.
21 If your enemy is hungry, give him food to eat;
And if he is thirsty, give him water to drink;
22 For you will heap burning coals on his head,
And the LORD will reward you.
23 The north wind brings forth rain,
And a backbiting tongue, an angry countenance.
24 It is better to live in a corner of the roof
Than in a house shared with a contentious woman.
25 *Like* cold water to a weary soul,
So is good news from a distant land.
26 *Like* a trampled spring and a polluted well
Is a righteous man who gives way before the wicked.
27 It is not good to eat much honey,
Nor is it glory to search out one's own glory.
28 *Like* a city that is broken into *and* without walls
Is a man who has no control over his spirit.

NOTES

Proverbs 25
~ Day ~

❖ Wisdom for Today

_____

_____

❖ Interpretation for Today

_____

_____

_____

_____

_____

❖ Strategy for Today

_____

_____

_____

_____

_____

Proverbs 25
~ Night ~

❖ Evaluation for Today

_____

_____

_____

_____

_____

_____

_____

_____

1 Like snow in summer and like rain in harvest,
So honor is not fitting for a fool.
2 Like a sparrow in *its* flitting, like a swallow in *its* flying,
So a curse without cause does not alight.
3 A whip is for the horse, a bridle for the donkey,
And a rod for the back of fools.
4 Do not answer a fool according to his folly,
Or you will also be like him.
5 Answer a fool as his folly *deserves,*
That he not be wise in his own eyes.
6 He cuts off *his own* feet *and* drinks violence
Who sends a message by the hand of a fool.
7 *Like* the legs *which* are useless to the lame,
So is a proverb in the mouth of fools.
8 Like one who binds a stone in a sling,
So is he who gives honor to a fool.
9 *Like* a thorn *which* falls into the hand of a drunkard,
So is a proverb in the mouth of fools.
10 *Like* an archer who wounds everyone,
So is he who hires a fool or who hires those who pass by.
11 Like a dog that returns to its vomit
Is a fool who repeats his folly.
12 Do you see a man wise in his own eyes?
There is more hope for a fool than for him.
13 The sluggard says, "There is a lion in the road!
A lion is in the open square!"
14 *As* the door turns on its hinges,
So *does* the sluggard on his bed.
15 The sluggard buries his hand in the dish;
He is weary of bringing it to his mouth again.
16 The sluggard is wiser in his own eyes
Than seven men who can give a discreet answer.
17 *Like* one who takes a dog by the ears
Is he who passes by *and* meddles with strife not belonging to him.

Proverbs 25
~ Day ~

❖ Wisdom for Today

_____

_____

❖ Interpretation for Today

_____

_____

_____

_____

_____

❖ Strategy for Today

_____

_____

_____

_____

_____

Proverbs 25
~ Night ~

❖ Evaluation for Today

_____

_____

_____

_____

_____

_____

_____

_____

18 Like a madman who throws
Firebrands, arrows and death,
19 So is the man who deceives his neighbor,
And says, "Was I not joking?"
20 For lack of wood the fire goes out,
And where there is no whisperer, contention quiets down.
21 *Like* charcoal to hot embers and wood to fire,
So is a contentious man to kindle strife.
22 The words of a whisperer are like dainty morsels,
And they go down into the innermost parts of the body.
23 *Like* an earthen vessel overlaid with silver dross
Are burning lips and a wicked heart.
24 He who hates disguises *it* with his lips,
But he lays up deceit in his heart.
25 When he speaks graciously, do not believe him,
For there are seven abominations in his heart.
26 *Though his* hatred covers itself with guile,
His wickedness will be revealed before the assembly.
27 He who digs a pit will fall into it,
And he who rolls a stone, it will come back on him.
28 A lying tongue hates those it crushes,
And a flattering mouth works ruin.

NOTES

Proverbs 26
~ Day ~

❖ Wisdom for Today

_____

_____

❖ Interpretation for Today

_____

_____

_____

_____

_____

❖ Strategy for Today

_____

_____

_____

_____

_____

Proverbs 26
~ Night ~

❖ Evaluation for Today

_____

_____

_____

_____

_____

_____

_____

¹ Do not boast about tomorrow,
For you do not know what a day may bring forth.
2 Let another praise you, and not your own mouth;
A stranger, and not your own lips.
3 A stone is heavy and the sand weighty,
But the provocation of a fool is heavier than both of them.
4 Wrath is fierce and anger is a flood,
But who can stand before jealousy?
5 Better is open rebuke
Than love that is concealed.
6 Faithful are the wounds of a friend,
But deceitful are the kisses of an enemy.
7 A sated man loathes honey,
But to a famished man any bitter thing is sweet.
8 Like a bird that wanders from her nest,
So is a man who wanders from his home.
9 Oil and perfume make the heart glad,
So a man's counsel is sweet to his friend.
10 Do not forsake your own friend or your father's friend,
And do not go to your brother's house in the day of your calamity;
Better is a neighbor who is near than a brother far away.
11 Be wise, my son, and make my heart glad,
That I may reply to him who reproaches me.
12 A prudent man sees evil *and* hides himself,
The naive proceed *and* pay the penalty.
13 Take his garment when he becomes surety for a
stranger; And for an adulterous woman hold him in pledge.
14 He who blesses his friend with a loud voice early in the
morning, It will be reckoned a curse to him.
15 A constant dripping on a day of steady rain
And a contentious woman are alike;
16 He who would restrain her restrains the wind,
And grasps oil with his right hand.

17 Iron sharpens iron, So one man sharpens another.
18 He who tends the fig tree will eat its fruit,
And he who cares for his master will be honored.
19 As in water face *reflects* face,
So the heart of man *reflects* man.
20 Sheol and Abaddon are never satisfied,
Nor are the eyes of man ever satisfied.
21 The crucible is for silver and the furnace for gold,
And each *is tested* by the praise accorded him.
22 Though you pound a fool in a mortar with a pestle along
with crushed grain,
Yet his foolishness will not depart from him.
23 Know well the condition of your flocks,
And pay attention to your herds;
24 For riches are not forever,
Nor does a crown *endure* to all generations.
25 *When* the grass disappears, the new growth is seen,
And the herbs of the mountains are gathered in,
26 The lambs *will be* for your clothing,
And the goats *will bring* the price of a field,
27 And *there will be* goats' milk enough for your food,
For the food of your household, And sustenance for your
maidens.

NOTES

Proverbs 27
~ Day ~

❖ Wisdom for Today

_____

_____

❖ Interpretation for Today

_____

_____

_____

_____

_____

❖ Strategy for Today

_____

_____

_____

_____

_____

Proverbs 27
~ Night ~

❖ Evaluation for Today

_____

_____

_____

_____

_____

_____

_____

Proverbs 28

1 The wicked flee when no one is pursuing,
But the righteous are bold as a lion.
2 By the transgression of a land many are its princes,
But by a man of understanding *and* knowledge, so it endures.
3 A poor man who oppresses the lowly
Is *like* a driving rain which leaves no food.
4 Those who forsake the law praise the wicked,
But those who keep the law strive with them.
5 Evil men do not understand justice,
But those who seek the LORD understand all things.
6 Better is the poor who walks in his integrity
Than he who is crooked though he be rich.
7 He who keeps the law is a discerning son,
But he who is a companion of gluttons humiliates his father.
8 He who increases his wealth by interest and usury
Gathers it for him who is gracious to the poor.
9 He who turns away his ear from listening to the law,
Even his prayer is an abomination.
10 He who leads the upright astray in an evil way
Will himself fall into his own pit,
But the blameless will inherit good.
11 The rich man is wise in his own eyes,
But the poor who has understanding sees through him.
12 When the righteous triumph, there is great glory,
But when the wicked rise, men hide themselves.
13 He who conceals his transgressions will not prosper,
But he who confesses and forsakes *them* will find compassion.
14 How blessed is the man who fears always,
But he who hardens his heart will fall into calamity.
15 *Like* a roaring lion and a rushing bear
Is a wicked ruler over a poor people.
16 A leader who is a great oppressor lacks understanding,
But he who hates unjust gain will prolong *his* days.
17 A man who is laden with the guilt of human blood
Will be a fugitive until death; let no one support him.

18 He who walks blamelessly will be delivered,
But he who is crooked will fall all at once.
19 He who tills his land will have plenty of food,
But he who follows empty *pursuits* will have poverty in plenty.
20 A faithful man will abound with blessings,
But he who makes haste to be rich will not go unpunished.
21 To show partiality is not good,
Because for a piece of bread a man will transgress.
22 A man with an evil eye hastens after wealth
And does not know that want will come upon him.
23 He who rebukes a man will afterward find *more* favor
Than he who flatters with the tongue.
24 He who robs his father or his mother
And says, "It is not a transgression,"
Is the companion of a man who destroys.
25 An arrogant man stirs up strife,
But he who trusts in the LORD will prosper.
26 He who trusts in his own heart is a fool,
But he who walks wisely will be delivered.
27 He who gives to the poor will never want,
But he who shuts his eyes will have many curses.
28 When the wicked rise, men hide themselves;
But when they perish, the righteous increase.

NOTES

Proverbs 28
~ Day ~

❖ Wisdom for Today

_____
_____

❖ Interpretation for Today

_____
_____
_____
_____
_____

❖ Strategy for Today

_____
_____
_____
_____
_____

Proverbs 28
~ Night ~

❖ Evaluation for Today

_____
_____
_____
_____
_____
_____
_____
_____

¹ A man who hardens *his* neck after much reproof
Will suddenly be broken beyond remedy.
2 When the righteous increase, the people rejoice,
But when a wicked man rules, people groan.
3 A man who loves wisdom makes his father glad,
But he who keeps company with harlots wastes *his* wealth.
4 The king gives stability to the land by justice,
But a man who takes bribes overthrows it.
5 A man who flatters his neighbor
Is spreading a net for his steps.
6 By transgression an evil man is ensnared,
But the righteous sings and rejoices.
7 The righteous is concerned for the rights of the poor,
The wicked does not understand *such* concern.
8 Scorners set a city aflame,
But wise men turn away anger.
9 When a wise man has a controversy with a foolish man,
The foolish man either rages or laughs, and there is no rest.
10 Men of bloodshed hate the blameless,
But the upright are concerned for his life.
11 A fool always loses his temper,
But a wise man holds it back.
12 If a ruler pays attention to falsehood,
All his ministers *become* wicked.
13 The poor man and the oppressor have this in common:
The LORD gives light to the eyes of both.
14 If a king judges the poor with truth,
His throne will be established forever.
15 The rod and reproof give wisdom,
But a child who gets his own way brings shame to his mother.
16 When the wicked increase, transgression increases;
But the righteous will see their fall.
17 Correct your son, and he will give you comfort;
He will also delight your soul.

18 Where there is no vision, the people are unrestrained,
But happy is he who keeps the law.
19 A slave will not be instructed by words *alone;*
For though he understands, there will be no response.
20 Do you see a man who is hasty in his words?
There is more hope for a fool than for him.
21 He who pampers his slave from childhood
Will in the end find him to be a son.
22 An angry man stirs up strife,
And a hot-tempered man abounds in transgression.
23 A man's pride will bring him low,
But a humble spirit will obtain honor.
24 He who is a partner with a thief hates his own life;
He hears the oath but tells nothing.
25 The fear of man brings a snare,
But he who trusts in the LORD will be exalted.
26 Many seek the ruler's favor,
But justice for man *comes* from the LORD.
27 An unjust man is abominable to the righteous,
And he who is upright in the way is abominable to the
wicked.

NOTES

Proverbs 29
~ Day ~

❖ Wisdom for Today

_____
_____

❖ Interpretation for Today

_____
_____
_____
_____
_____

❖ Strategy for Today

_____
_____
_____
_____
_____

Proverbs 29
~ Night ~

❖ Evaluation for Today

_____
_____
_____
_____
_____
_____
_____
_____

Proverbs 30

1 The words of Agur the son of Jakeh, the oracle.
The man declares to Ithiel, to Ithiel and Ucal:
2 Surely I am more stupid than any man,
And I do not have the understanding of a man.
3 Neither have I learned wisdom,
Nor do I have the knowledge of the Holy One.
4 Who has ascended into heaven and descended?
Who has gathered the wind in His fists?
Who has wrapped the waters in His garment?
Who has established all the ends of the earth?
What is His name or His son's name? Surely you know!
5 Every word of God is tested;
He is a shield to those who take refuge in Him.
6 Do not add to His words
Or He will reprove you, and you will be proved a liar.
7 Two things I asked of You,
Do not refuse me before I die:
8 Keep deception and lies far from me,
Give me neither poverty nor riches;
Feed me with the food that is my portion,
9 That I not be full and deny *You* and say, "Who is the LORD?" Or
that I not be in want and steal,
And profane the name of my God.
10 Do not slander a slave to his master,
Or he will curse you and you will be found guilty.
11 There is a kind of *man* who curses his father
And does not bless his mother.
12 There is a kind who is pure in his own eyes,
Yet is not washed from his filthiness.
13 There is a kind--oh how lofty are his eyes!
And his eyelids are raised *in arrogance.*
14 There is a kind of *man* whose teeth are *like* swords
And his jaw teeth *like* knives,
To devour the afflicted from the earth
And the needy from among men.
15 The leech has two daughters, "Give," "Give." There are three
things that will not be satisfied, Four that will not say, "Enough":

16 Sheol, and the barren womb,
Earth that is never satisfied with water,
And fire that never says, "Enough."
17 The eye that mocks a father And scorns a mother,
The ravens of the valley will pick it out,
And the young eagles will eat it.
18 There are three things which are too wonderful for me, Four
which I do not understand:
19 The way of an eagle in the sky,
The way of a serpent on a rock, The way of a ship in the middle of
the sea, And the way of a man with a maid.
20 This is the way of an adulterous woman: She eats and wipes her
mouth, And says, "I have done no wrong."
21 Under three things the earth quakes,
And under four, it cannot bear up:
22 Under a slave when he becomes king,
And a fool when he is satisfied with food,
23 Under an unloved woman when she gets a husband,
And a maidservant when she supplants her mistress.
24 Four things are small on the earth,
But they are exceedingly wise:
25 The ants are not a strong people,
But they prepare their food in the summer;
26 The shephanim are not mighty people,
Yet they make their houses in the rocks;
27 The locusts have no king, Yet all of them go out in ranks;
28 The lizard you may grasp with the hands,
Yet it is in kings' palaces.
29 There are three things which are stately in *their* march,
Even four which are stately when they walk:
30 The lion *which* is mighty among beasts
And does not retreat before any,
31 The strutting rooster, the male goat also,
And a king *when his* army is with him.
32 If you have been foolish in exalting yourself
Or if you have plotted *evil, put your* hand on your mouth.
33 For the churning of milk produces butter,
And pressing the nose brings forth blood;
So the churning of anger produces strife

NOTES

Proverbs 30
~ Day ~

❖ Wisdom for Today

_____

_____

❖ Interpretation for Today

_____

_____

_____

_____

_____

❖ Strategy for Today

_____

_____

_____

_____

_____

Proverbs 30
~ Night ~

❖ Evaluation for Today

_____

_____

_____

_____

_____

_____

_____

_____

¹ The words of King Lemuel,
the oracle which his mother taught him:
2 What, O my son?
And what, O son of my womb?
And what, O son of my vows?
3 Do not give your strength to women,
Or your ways to that which destroys kings.
4 It is not for kings, O Lemuel,
It is not for kings to drink wine,
Or for rulers to desire strong drink,
5 For they will drink and forget what is decreed,
And pervert the rights of all the afflicted.
6 Give strong drink to him who is perishing,
And wine to him whose life is bitter.
7 Let him drink and forget his poverty
And remember his trouble no more.
8 Open your mouth for the mute,
For the rights of all the unfortunate.
9 Open your mouth, judge righteously,
And defend the rights of the afflicted and needy.
Description of a Worthy Woman
10 An excellent wife, who can find?
For her worth is far above jewels.
11 The heart of her husband trusts in her,
And he will have no lack of gain.
12 She does him good and not evil
All the days of her life.
13 She looks for wool and flax
And works with her hands in delight.
14 She is like merchant ships;
She brings her food from afar.
15 She rises also while it is still night
And gives food to her household
And portions to her maidens.

16 She considers a field and buys it;
From her earnings she plants a vineyard.
17 She girds herself with strength
And makes her arms strong.
18 She senses that her gain is good;
Her lamp does not go out at night.
19 She stretches out her hands to the distaff,
And her hands grasp the spindle.
20 She extends her hand to the poor,
And she stretches out her hands to the needy.
21 She is not afraid of the snow for her household,
For all her household are clothed with scarlet.
22 She makes coverings for herself;
Her clothing is fine linen and purple.
23 Her husband is known in the gates,
When he sits among the elders of the land.
24 She makes linen garments and sells *them,*
And supplies belts to the tradesmen.
25 Strength and dignity are her clothing,
And she smiles at the future.
26 She opens her mouth in wisdom,
And the teaching of kindness is on her tongue.
27 She looks well to the ways of her household,
And does not eat the bread of idleness.
28 Her children rise up and bless her;
Her husband *also,* and he praises her, *saying:*
29 "Many daughters have done nobly,
But you excel them all."
30 Charm is deceitful and beauty is vain,
But a woman who fears the LORD, she shall be praised.
31 Give her the product of her hands,
And let her works praise her in the gates.

NOTES

NOTES

Proverbs 31
~ Day ~

❖ Wisdom for Today

_____

_____

❖ Interpretation for Today

_____

_____

_____

_____

_____

❖ Strategy for Today

_____

_____

_____

_____

_____

Proverbs 31
~ Night ~

❖ Evaluation for Today

_____

_____

_____

_____

_____

_____

_____

Know well the condition of your flocks,
And pay attention to your herds

~ Proverbs 27:23

The Wisdom Journal
Monthly Summary

www.wisdomjournal.org

NOTES

The Wisdom Journal Monthly Summary

MONTH_____YEAR_____

Reflect on your successes and your victories this month!

_____
_____
_____
_____
_____
_____
_____
_____
_____
_____
_____
_____
_____
_____
_____
_____
_____
_____
_____
_____
_____
_____
_____
_____
_____
_____
_____

The Wisdom Search

Over 100 times the words wisdom & wise are used in the Book of Proverbs. Discover each wisdom verse as your journey begins and write your verses below.

1.	19.	37.	55.	73.	91.
2.	20.	38.	56.	74.	92.
3.	21.	39.	57.	75.	93.
4.	22.	40.	58.	76.	94.
5.	23.	41.	59.	77.	95.
6.	24.	42.	60.	78.	96.
7.	25.	43.	61.	79.	97.
8.	26.	44.	62.	80.	98.
9.	27.	45.	63.	81.	99.
10.	28.	46.	64.	82.	100.
11.	29.	47.	65.	83.	101.
12.	30.	48.	66.	84.	102.
13.	31.	49.	67.	85.	103.
14.	32.	50.	68.	86.	104.
15.	33.	51.	69.	87.	105.
16.	34.	52.	70.	88.	106.
17.	35.	53.	71.	89.	107.
18.	36.	54.	72.	90.	108.

Conclusion of The Matter

Fear God, and keep his commandments;
for this is the whole duty of man.

Ecclesiastes 12:13

www.wisdomjournal.org

Wisdom's instruction is to fear the Lord
And humility comes before honor

~ Proverbs 15:33

www.wisdomjournal.org
CONGRATULATIONS!
ANOTHER MONTH OF WISDOM

FOR COPIES OF THE WISDOM JOURNAL
SUBSCRIBE FOR MONTHLY JOURNAL DELIVERY
ORDER JOURNALS FOR SMALL GROUP BIBLE STUDY
PARTICIPATE IN AN UPCOMING WISDOM WORKSHOP
JOIN MONTHLY WISDOM FOR LIFE MASTERMIND GROUP

www.wisdomjournal.org or call 561-309-1334.

To Contact Marc Feinberg

Personal Advisor, Performance Expert
Author & Keynote Speaker

Call 561-309-1334

Email: info@thewisdomgroup.org

Marc Feinberg
"The Wisdom Guy"

Marc Feinberg is a Lifestyle Entrepreneur for over 30 years and a Certified Biblical Counselor for over 20 years. He is also a High-Performance Coach & Personal Advisor to some of the Highest Achieving Athletes and Entrepreneurs all across the world. (**www.marcfeinberg.com**)

Marc grew up Jewish in Queens NY, got Bar Mitzvah at 13 years old in the summer of 1977, and then he gave his life to Jesus Christ at 31 years old at Calvary Chapel FT Lauderdale on Jan 7, 1996.

He wakes up every day on a mission to build bridges, stand in the gap, and to move his clients into their highest purpose & possibility, which he also refers to as their TRUTH.

Marc's greatest passion is to teach wisdom from the Book of Proverbs, and… to equip God's people for works of service, so that the body of Christ may be built up until we all reach unity in the faith and in the knowledge of the Son of God and become mature, attaining to the whole measure of the fullness of Christ.

Marc's message to people all across the world is simple… YOU are the New Prophet in the world today. YOUR life experience & YOUR life lessons contain the necessary wisdom to help others live a victorious Spirit-filled life.

Read YOUR Proverb today & "Stay WISE my Friends."
Marc Feinberg

Made in the USA
Middletown, DE
26 May 2024

54751250R00103